Still and Still Moving

"With *Still and Still Moving*, Katie Scruggs Galloway is a curator of moments, finding vibrant life in the smallest details. Her talent for observation transports the reader to a world of pastel clocks and coffee-stained roses, where time is a suggestion more than an inevitability. It is here in this world where she plants a flowerbed of earnest promises and sepia-toned references, waiting for a spring that may never come; but the joy is in the gardening."

— Renzo Del Castillo,
Author of *Still*

"Galloway's *Still and Still Moving* contains some of the most vivid and mesmerizing poetry I have read in a long time. Every poem and photograph brought me to a different world—one of thought-provoking joy and love-driven despair. *Still and Still Moving* is a collection of poetry that I am sure I will read over and over, learning something new each time. Galloway's poetry cannot be missed."

— Kristen Noelle Richards,
Author of *as if to return myself to the sea*

"*Still and Still Moving* is a beautiful, intimate exploration of the self, demonstrated through curated pairings of photos, collages, and typewritten drafts with deftly written poems that inquire and respond to memories. Galloway has crafted a hauntingly gorgeous hybrid poetry collection that is deeply personal but lingers and resonates universally."

— Tanya Sangpun Thamkruphat,
Author of *Em(body)ment of Wonder* and *It Wasn't a Dream*

"A beautiful and contemplative reflection of the preservation of memories, raw emotions, and vulnerability. Galloway weaves lyrical imagery through honest prose in a search for time, truth, love, and the many shades of blue."

— Marisa S. White,
Fine Art Photographer

"In the quiet spaces between words and the gentle rhythm of life, Katie Scruggs Galloway's *Still and Still Moving* invites us to pause and savor everyday beauty. With a masterful touch, she weaves a tapestry of emotions and observations. Her poems are like snapshots of the human experience, capturing moments of vulnerability, joy, and reflection with a grace that is both raw and tender. *Still and Still Moving* is an ode to the ordinary and a testament to Galloway's talent and her ability to find magic in the mundane."
— Leah Noel Moon,
Author of *Caprice*

"*Still and Still Moving* is a symphony that sings each emotion, thought, and experience in its own perfect melody. Beauty is laid onto each page with outstanding visuals that pair with Galloway's words in unexpected ways. These poems encapsulate more than you think you can ever know. An outstanding read."
— Amelie Honeysuckle,
Author of *What Once Was An Inside Out Rainbow*

"*Still and Still Moving* drags you forward while your knuckles and claws beat on the door of memory—always out of reach, yet always haunting. If you want to feel a cathartic release, want to feel understood in that dance between yearning for the past, fear of the future, and hope for the present, this is a lovely read to carry you through those troubled waters."
— Brandon Flanery,
Author of *Stumbling*

"*Still and Still Moving* makes my soul feel like it can take a peaceful breath among the pastel clouds. It calls attention to human needs and actions that many people tend to overlook. Stunning imagery and beautiful words carry me gently among these pages. Galloway allows me to be still, while still moving."
— Kendall Hope,
Author of *The Willow Weepings*

Still and Still Moving

Poems

Katie Scruggs Galloway

INDIE EARTH
PUBLISHING

Cover Art Copyright © 2023 by Katie Scruggs Galloway
Photography Copyright © 2023 by Katie Scruggs Galloway and Marisa S. White
Edited by Flor Ana Mireles

1st Edition | 01
Hardcover ISBN: 979-8-9862106-7-4
Paperback ISBN: 979-8-9890939-1-5

First Published October 2023

For inquiries and bulk orders, please email:
indieearthbooks@gmail.com

Printed in the United States of America   1 2 3 4 5 6 7 8 9

Indie Earth Publishing Inc.
| Miami, FL |

www.indieearthbooks.com

"We must be still and still moving
Into another intensity
For a further union, a deeper communion
Through the dark cold and the empty desolation,
The wave cry, the wind cry, the vast waters
Of the petrel and the porpoise.
In my end is my beginning."

– T. S. Eliot
East Coker, The Four Quartets

CONTENTS

"We must be still
and still moving
Into another intensity."
                    T.S. Eliot

SECTION ONE

The Past Is a Balloon

WHO DO YOU STILL LOVE?

People swirl as if dancing to a song only they can hear. Can you hear it? The words mean nothing. It's more rhythm than rhetoric. And no one pays attention anyway.

They talk over the outro fade and pretend the end won't come. When it does, we lean into the chatter—contributing small nothings to replace discomfort. The lights, neon. The laughs, neurotic. The liturgies, nagging.

With eyes half open, I search faces like they hold clues to a crossword. Their vocabulary is just on the edge of my vernacular. My cheeks blush a pink like the underbelly of a puppy you loved and still love. Who do you still love?

PASTEL CLOCKS

Flowers used to be just flowers. But here, on the kitchen table, are white roses turned the color of a coffee stain. A coffee stain on your white-collared shirt, the one ironed in a hurry, sloppily, for now no good reason.

In this moment (and other moments more and more often), flowers are little pastel clocks pointing me to the unwanted wisdom that I cannot contain time. Each fiery bloom is illuminated by whatever beauty burns up as fuel. But the bulb does burn out. I will never be able to see again the sunrise that made me cry that summer in Tucson on a rooftop with my sister. And anyway,

the sign in your garden that says "please no peeing" is (I promise you) much less attractive than whatever you're worried will happen to your flower beds if your neighbor lets his Boykin Spaniel piss in your yard. But I can understand the sentiment. The sign, stakes dug deep in the ground, and I share the same wish on a petal:

Please don't accelerate the inevitable decay.

Is all my life an unsuccessful effort to reverse entropy? Eyes on the clock. Hands busy holding browning petals. A shirt soaked in bleach. It's possible.

But it's possible the stain will lift.

A HOPE TO BE HEARD

We walk backwards, listening with piqued ears to the music we missed out on while we were busy making jokes we are embarrassed by now. Why are my cheeks always hot? Isn't regeneration what we hope for? I don't want to be who I was yesterday, but is it so wrong to feel that I don't want to burn her? I want to remember. Remember when I was learning how to swing? My legs pumping fast back and forth, back and forth, while my head turned left and right (left and right) wondering why my brother and sister found flying so easy. This is the first comparison. Jealousy as a bright green leaf.

And there were leaves growing on a single sunflower in the backyard, still so small. In the early morning, I sang spontaneous songs from the swing set into that microphone of gold. From the beginning, I wanted my words to have some reach. From the beginning, I sang hoping you would hear me. Who instructed me? I don't remember learning to sing; it required no confused pumping of the feet, invited no jealousy.

Now driving down I-24, I sing soaked in salt. Words steam up the windshield. Are you still listening? I run through the doorways in my memory, desperate for that sliding glass that will welcome me back to a patch of grass—back to those yellow petals; a hope to be heard.

EVIDENCE

I look for evidence that my life is not a photograph. The invasive gust of wind tangling my hair. The clang of a wind chime from the neighbor's yard. I want to see and hear and feel my experience returned to me, even if only in ceramic bells.

Shadows change direction, stretching and shortening, stretching again. The reach and recoil. There is the stillness. And then there is what moves over that stillness. There is movement, but is there a way to move closer?

The mirage shimmers, consistent only in the distance it keeps from me.

PLAYING ALCHEMIST

Trying now to recall pictures of hope, they look like photo negatives. All light and shadows. Compressed into the two dimensions of reductionist reasoning. I spend my mornings trying to channel sunlight through a lens to enlarge the scaffolding of possibility I've convinced myself is locked in the past.

Afternoons are spent searching under the cupboards for chemicals. I play alchemist until the sun sets, imagining what might resurface on the photosensitive paper. I look up, unsure where the light went.

Another day is archived. Car lights shine through the street-facing windows. They flicker like laughter, a teasing kind. I pull back the blinds, my hands pressed against the windowpane. I beg the daylight of yesterday to make some kind of re-entry, to return. Or else take me along.

AN OBLIVION LIKE BLASPHEMY

I try to learn something from Woolf's searching. And then I learn something from her resignation. Isn't it meant to be obvious? Shouldn't those who seek find? I find more questions on the tail end of each answer. That tired dog still chasing his tail, unaware that it is right there where it has always been . . .

Where did I leave him? Can I leave him at all? Can a resident of the heart still miss calls? I should be falling in love with Jesus, I know. But each week I fall more in love with Paul Buchanan. An oblivion like blasphemy resonates as a base line so heavy it sticks like gum to the shoe. *I will never leave you or forsake you.* But why can't I hear you? *The coffee's cold and out of reach.* But why am I still reaching? You are mistaken. I hope I'm mistaken.

STILL HERE

I speak to you in tongues, too afraid of what I might admit in my native language. Now choreographing dances around the object of my apprehension, I pretend they are letters sent with no return address. I pretend I cannot be found.

I call a friend so he can convince me why I should not mourn a life I am still living. *Still,* the past is a balloon that has floated to the ceiling. My arms are in constant extension, relentless reaching. Whatever the present tense throws my way falls through arms that have forgotten how to bend, how to hold, how to *embrace.*

You ask me how I'm doing these days, and I try to find an inconspicuous way to say I'm on the shadow side of fine. That fragility is all I'm sure of. The only flag I can remember how to wave is of quilted caution tape. Have I forgotten surrender?

The dew of distance between lovers covers us like summer sweat. It is like a sheet you can't kick off in the night. The linens tangled around your feet, uncomfortable. *You* are uncomfortable. And I'm apologetic. I am the half-broken fan that doesn't oscillate like it used to. Despite my injury, I try to offer a cool kiss, a hand across the center console, a touch that says, I'm sorry. *But I'm still here.*

A TOO BRIGHT TUNGSTEN LIGHT

Goodbye is an infection my body never grows immune to. Thirsty from fever, I drink in the sound of your laughter and try to be as well as I can be. Does it ever get easier? To love? To leave? To be anything other than desperate to touch yesterday?

I am alone in a bed made up for two, wondering who I might be without you. The tapes of my memory wear thin, and I'm clinging to the scraps, stretching my eyes to somehow see past this present sick bed and remember when, remember when, remember when . . .

FEEDBACK LOOP

the field of memory is full of land-mines to walk through. Wake early, engine running, humming its tune. The new morning clouds look like birthday balloons tied to a chair. The mind is a doorway, and the subconscious, a room. Outside,

Your friends and family are already there. Beyond the mind is a door-way, and the subconscious, a room. Outside, the field of memory is full of landmines to walk through.

THE FOSSILS I FIND

Restlessness pushed me out my front door. But it was the cold that pushed me to the sunny side of the street. Spring is a coward. Trees wait barren, apprehensive of an April snow. I struggle to pick my eyes up off the ground. The cracks of the sidewalk become mile markers. I count them out of impulse, replicating the ticks of the clock, which has lost its importance in this age we are reminded: death does not wear a watch.

I try to walk slowly, making negotiations with my heart rate. Bargaining for ease. I heard in a song once, *there's no place to get to / lovers don't forget you / hello*—Hello. I am greeted by [the impression of] a leaf. A record of what used to be cast in the cold concrete, a modern fossil.

So, not all will be forgotten? I smile at the possibility of preservation. I write another something down, hoping the leaves of paper scribbled with reminders will lead me back to whatever idolized past I need, when I need it, or else some imagined future—concrete that is still wet.

SECTION TWO

Where I End and Artifact Begins

SWAYED JUDGMENT

Idioms are rewritten by the kids who couldn't tie their shoes when we were graduating high school. The fox's oath is pet-named fake news. The rooster's tail is filed with the receipts. Still, in the middle of meaning's shape-shifting performance, understanding remains: *there's good reason to be skeptical.*

Understanding hides in the offbeat. This offbeat is intended for swaying (not clapping—better not to shout what you're not sure of). It is the space for movement between ticks of the metronome. Understanding is not a box you must fold in upon yourself to fit inside. It is a dance. A dance in which we are all moving closer.

IS, NOT: KEY

Truth waits for me, not like my father after curfew. Truth waits for me like the needle waits to be placed on a record. Truth is both the waiting and what we are all waiting for. Both music and silence. A song.

I wait to hear it, antsy for the intro. I want your words to drip onto the tip of my head like a hot shower after another feverish night, heartbeat heavy and loud from dreams turned sour. I want the welcomed comfort of your nearness. I want your voice like it's the first-chair violinist's tuning note. A mess made beautiful in the amphitheater: I want the symphony to begin.

MUSIC EDUCATION

There began the summer of music education. Springsteen singing over a warm static, buzzing in my earbuds before I am. I am climbing into a '69 Chevy, driving down the strip. From the passenger seat, I watch the window, press my hand to the glass. *Here I am.* It's a half-question. From the outside, I look into the night. The night. *I wish this night was electric.* Is the summer really here? Pictures of my grandfather's Daytona yellow Camaro flash in my mind. Why is it easier to remember the black leather seats, dusted by Arizona, than it is to remember his voice? His voice is always drenched in nostalgia. Or regret. Isn't it both? The guitar is only trying to emulate the same effect. *We are waiting for the time to be right.* Waiting to find out whatever happened to the dude from LA. How much longer will my hands bleed from stitching up torn pretty dreams? Will there always be more repairs? More to fix, everything but the head gasket. Did my grandfather love the work of a mechanic? Or did he just love cars? Maybe both. Maybe he and I wanted and want only to go racing in the street.

FALL, UNSUSPECTING

June was a match that burned quickly, nipping at my fingertips with little teeth of heat. There was nothing to do except watch its brief glow.

The ceiling drips, and no one stops to notice it—until someone slips, until the consequence is big enough. Is it enough to see one thread through? To live, and walk, and fall—unsuspecting. No one watched the puddle form, but aren't we responsible for even the (so-called) inconsequential?

june
was a match
that burned
quickly.

THE HUNT

I recall now the conversation we had about the fear I feel when I walk through a museum. At some point I lose track of where I end and artifact begins. There was something else, something about glass boxes. And how I'm not ready for my memories to require active preservation. But they already do. There is a whole world I feel unready to lose. Have I already lost you?

I feel like a small child on Easter with lace socks and no basket. I fill my arms with pastel memories like little plastic eggs. There are too many of them. As I bend to pick up another, two fall back on the ground, half-hidden in the uncut grass. Some observing adult giggles behind my back. Aren't you all giggling behind my back? I can't blame you.

But you can't blame me for joining the hunt.

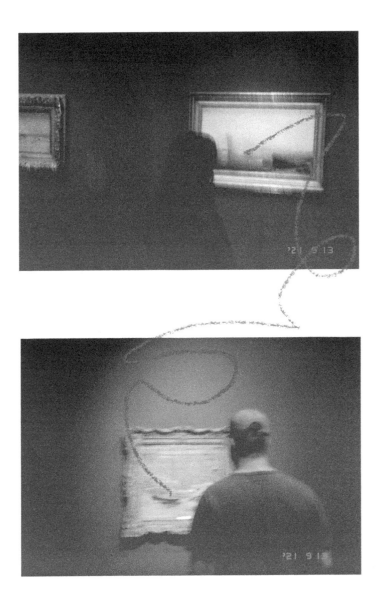

REVOLVING

I thought that a helicopter was hovering overhead, but it was just the machines in the walls. Have they been working while we weren't watching? From the backyard we share, I can see the rooftop of Memorial Hospital. Life flights happen every hour, it feels like. The revolving spins me into a swirl of anxiety I remember from adolescence. *It's just the machines within my walls.* Just the *memory* of fear. Still, it's unclear how to distinguish the difference. When the revolving starts, I can't fight the urge to duck and cover.

Drafts

I reread my childhood favorites, looking for ~~some~~ truth I must have overlooked. Why am I still trying to synthesize someone else's story to make some sense of my own? Even in hindsight, my life is a series of unfinished diary entires spread across many notebooks ~~house~~ upon many shelves--the meaning scattered.

The dude fom LA calls to share a new record with me, he asks why I keep so much guilt in my back pocket or why I keep it at all. I have no answers. We discuss the lights we see as the songs change shape. *Don't we all see something?* A passing light. I want badly to be honest. *Is this the life you always wanted?* Yes. Yes, absolutely, but I wanted so many others too.

I reconstruct apology letters from lyrics I know you'll recognize. You will, won't you?

k. galloway
September 21, 2020

DRAFTS

I reread my childhood favorites, to find some truth I must have overlooked. Why am I still trying to synthesize someone else's story to make sense of my own? Even in hindsight, my life is a series of unfinished diary entries spread across many notebooks upon many shelves—the meaning scattered.

I reconstruct apology letters from lyrics I know you'll recognize. You will, won't you?

The dude from LA calls to share a new record with me. He asks why I keep so much guilt in my back pocket or why I keep it at all. I have no answers. We discuss the lights we see as the songs change shape. *Don't we all see something?* A passing light. I want badly to be honest. *Is this the life you always wanted?* Yes. Yes, absolutely, but I wanted so many others too.

VERTIGO

Again at the intersections. The music fell between the genres. Faith now feels less like obliging to the silent nod that ends an argument and more like choosing to fall. The days lose their dimension under the distortion of vertigo. Slight noises set me on edge, and I wish my ears were not as the windmill in the yard, so in need of oil. It cries at the smallest prodding, the push of a breeze.

I crave stillness. The contradictions meet: I want to evolve, but I am afraid of what's around the bend. Beyond the horizon. Beyond the sea. What is it you see in me?

When the words finally cease, I worry what that might mean for my prayers. Some days feel like falling into a bed of static, and my mind half-inhabits two planes with sounds in frequencies that cancel one another out. Where am I supposed to go now?

THE SOUND OF DEPARTURES

I remember hearing your voice in my head while I read novels in high school. Is that why I've been in the habit of rereading? I reread the red letters too. *Speak up, I'm losing you.* Keaton sings his prayer. His voice, too, is a thread between my past lives and this present condition.

In this present condition, my ears are overwhelmed by the sound of departures. It's that helicopter again. Voices shouting—their goodbyes strain over the machines. I can't hear anything.

BEFORE THE TAPE WAS RECORDED OVER

What I'm trying to get across is, I don't like how many questions I've been presented with and how few answers I feel confident enough to give. Where's that little girl in the hot pink tank top who said, "*Dad,* this is supposed to be an adventure"? Was that it? Why can't I remember what I whined before the tape was recorded over? Why is my mind like a tape that can be recorded over?

I want the world to be backed up on a hard drive. It would have as many terabytes as there are stars in the galaxies. In other words, capacity would never be an issue. The contents would be orderly, and we would always know just where to go to find what we want like we did in the grocery store of our hometown before they rearranged it. Why do they keep rearranging it?

READ ALOUD

The curtains are drawn, but I consider opening them to let the bright white of morning light fires in my irises and make a parchment of pain that I might be able to read aloud when you ask again, *How are you doing?* It's getting harder to exist, mostly because I fear the alternative. I'm afraid my life will end abruptly, like one of Salinger's stories. I'm afraid for you too. I know you've been low. But I still think, or hope, that you stand a chance of being a man with all his faculties intact.

Now I'm overwhelmed by my mortality. I weep into my husband's chest while he reminds me to make the best of what we've got. *This moment is all I have.* I despise the relentless advertising. And I marvel at you. Underneath my marveling is more anger. And all my anger is rooted in confusion.

I watch you as you snap photos without removing the lens cap. I want to snatch the camera back. I want to scold you for wasting a frame, for wasting so many days, for being so willing to give your life away. And for what reason?

READ LETTERS

I.

How can we see ourselves until we have been seen? He calls me Ultramarine. *Beyond the sea.* But the other side is so hard to see.

When I set the books down, I start to feel as if I'm living inside a painting. I look around for strokes of that coveted blue. Like clues, I piece them together. Arrows pointing always forward, even as they point to the past.

II.

Behold, I am doing a new thing; now it springs forth, do you not perceive it?

I reassure myself this must be the only way through. But I still struggle to find you, in red letters, in black letters, in the language-less strokes of precious paint. In this desert, I see blue only on the horizon. *Speak up, I'm losing you.* I step closer, I think. Only for the horizon to find a new beginning. *I will make a way in the wilderness and rivers in the desert.*

But night falls, and it takes even the horizon with it. I hold frames to my eyes, drawing perspective lines: a map still making. The backdrop is a shadow. I feel unable to cross. A standstill. A red light [red letters; read letters]. An opportunity half-lost. But what waits for me on the other side of the sea? If I make it there, who will I be? I know, my steps have always been small, but every movement is progress, even a crawl. I drag my feet in the sand and hear whispers on the edge of earshot. *Speak up.*

be still

　　　and know

　　　and go
　　　on to bed

　　　and still
　　　moving

　　　. . .

SECTION THREE

Wanting to Want to Praise

DOG-EARED MEMORY

I wake in the night to pull books from my shelves, looking for that dog-eared memory that will fill all the blank, black spaces between these daydreams. Eyes closed. Closer now I think either to savior or sorrow, I'm not yet sure. And I still desire certainty. I still flip back pages, waiting for that past-self signal, underlining in pencil, a trail back home.

Last night I dreamt that your new name was Night Train. My waking mind is embarrassed by the connotations. I want to erase all the marks I made about you before and let you reread the story uninformed.

Still, you are a vehicle of homecoming for so many. For me. For some reason, I feel like a child tracing over dotted cursive letters. Whose handwriting am I emulating? My hands have trouble learning new patterns. I guess the mind does too. It's obvious, isn't it? In every page, I'm looking for you. These days feel like learning to read in the dark, or else learning to do without reading. In the belly of a whale, there are no lamps. At least, always, a second second chance.

A night train, still on the way.

I STILL AM

I bite into, I chew, I regurgitate the Psalms. And somehow this does not feel like a bad thing. It is half-nourishing. But still half-disappointing. Wasn't I born into the second volume? I thought you said it was *finished*. But I find endless beginnings and always another flimsy resolution.

Suppose I find what I am looking for. Do the days still feel like loose threads pulled looser, pulled out? Whoever said they wanted freedom, I disagree with them now. I want to be woven into some story, some body, some beginning that never does find an end. Will I find an end?

In Sunday school a woman with brushed curls taught me to love what I couldn't see. I was enamored then by light. I still am. But tired, too, of chasing a setting sun.

THE EDGES OF TRADITION

Maybe maturity then is learning to love the mystery. I can come to no better conclusions. Not right now, anyway. The present is a pair of glasses with a prescription that's all wrong; I wonder what kind of fool hindsight will make of me. I lift my hands again to sing, wanting to want to praise. But it's not the same. I am still reaching for balloons that are still floating away. I strain to see them, to see you, to see something familiar, feeling my way along the edges of a tradition. Home is hardly recognizable.

IN

        that once-was ocean,
in arizona, the sky dies bright blue.
ultramarine--another crowded-mouth key:

a key that cuts;
~~on the shore i leave behind me,~~
~~or maybe only *that* i leave.~~

sky turned sea
~~ultramarine~~

if you had to go alone, would you still
come?

~~is this enough??~~
~~is this enough?~~
~~is this~~

60

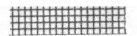

in arizona, that once-was ocean, the
sky dies bright blue. sky turned sea.
ultramarine--another crowded-mouth key.

a key that cuts:

if you had to go alone, would you
still come?

----
the last window
k. galloway
12/24/20

ONLY BLUE

The dusk becomes the dawn, and it's the only blue I want to bathe in. A lingering light; or an anticipated arrival. A return I trust will come; a light that never left—only eclipsed my view.

My view is made of many sharp corners. Rectangles over squares. The sheet of paper. The deep desk. The window. They are all perimeter, boundary, but within me, decision takes the shape of a spiral: one winding line that points ever-inward, a contrast image. A split second between "should do" and "I choose."

HOLD, HAPPILY

From the corner booth, I watch the man in the ball cap half-run, half-fall down the stairs, and I wonder where or who he's hurrying to. Are you hurrying too? The days feel shorter, but the weeks feel longer. And somehow months fall away like loose eyelashes no one got to wish on.

Is stillness really a steady hand [dancing on the edge of my depth of field]? My hands wax pensive, and I can't change the shutter speed. I square my eye with the viewfinder and try not to miss another moment. I try to hold, happily, the bliss, the blur, the blinding beginning beyond the bereaved.

ENTRANCE RAMP

So I make my bed in the curve of a question mark and nestle in to rest. I remember my head against the window, sitting on a bus bench, looking out at all my longings like my mother before me—we wanted everything. It is the most holy kind of greed, to acknowledge a need and feed it with promise, to endure, knowing the heart will not be forgotten.

Time is a string that stitches me to an ancestry in earnest. The wisdom of generations. Sewn into a quilt—the quilt I warm myself with, here, in the questions still.

And maybe persistence is a puzzle, I fool myself into playing. A patchwork of parts. Maybe persistence is a prayer, and in faith, I'm staying.

THE 405

Maybe it was just that I hadn't listened to the radio in some years, but I felt as though the 405 was escorting me into a future that [was for me, yet] had nothing to do with me: a surprise party planned by a stranger.

The ad readers rattle off conditions at a speed like falling and in a tone like an attempt to whisper over club music. A stifled shout. Without the perspective of the Rockies around me, I felt so much closer to the clouds. Of course, the opposite was true. Feelings were the first liars, and that's a lie too.

An old friend uses new words to tell me what we've known for years. We wonder, *How did we end up here?* And we know, not how to explain it, but that it'll be the same thing that gets us where we're going—a highway built before we were born.

WHOSE HOMECOMING

So the door *does* open. We stand squaring shoulders to better take in familiar faces through the frame of change. I get a good look at you—And your eyes answer questions before they have time to form on my lips. My lips start an "I love you," but the mind makes edits.

Instead, an "I see you" echoes off the shape of your expression. But aren't we standing in *my* kitchen? Why is a dream dreamt in the day so prone to shape-shifting? Why is it *me* who comes through your door so sure you're on the other side? I kick my heels to the corner and fall onto the couch. It's you who's in the kitchen now.

"I remember" is a blanket that keeps my love warm. And all joy I know now is laced in memory. How had I forgotten? That you're the same person I knew as a child, the one I whispered to on the playground. Now like it never left, I feel the safety of turning the knob, knowing the door is unlocked, of asking, knowing an answer waits—is this what my father called faith? That word that lights the fires of my embarrassment [the heat in my cheeks].

Still, I'm reclined on your couch. My fingernails trace lines in the polyester. The bottle of merlot empties like sand from an hourglass. Half empty. Half full. And again my cheeks are rosy, but it's the heat of memory, the blanket around my love, an audible "I remember"—the joy of homecoming.

NEW ROUTINE

The year goes on, and I learn to believe without satisfying the compulsion to find someone to agree with me. I let love be enough.

I let hope fall from cliché like powdered sugar through a sieve. I eat french toast every Sunday. I don't bother reframing anything that embarrasses me.

I lay in the sun. I let it burn. I watch clouds move slowly across the ocean of the sky. I ask again for the meaning of Ultramarine. I laugh loudly

when the question is returned.

I offer up the purest blue I can. All the honesty I have, laid out in a color unignorable.

There it is.
The truth: that bridge I was so scared to cross.

© *Somewhere by Marisa S. White*
marisaswhite.com

STURDY IS THE DOORFRAME,
FLUID ARE THE SANDS

instinct moves through me
simple as
a door left open
my arm's subconscious extension
reaches out
to brace the fall
or else feel for
another way to be.

my fingertips trace the shape
of messages left in the mirror
s l o w
      condensation
now reconnection
slow condensation
now
      reconnection
I hear it echo in our teenage voices
and realize,
or remember,
the sacred loves to speak
our unique languages.

instinct moves through me
simple as
a native tongue
they say

what we seek
we find
our eyes
half-blinded
from fixating on a certain light
the silhouette of it
burned into our vision
like an omen
the shape of the puzzle piece
not yet found.

I used to walk to the horizon line.
following a fading light
these days,
I love a vertical line,
the glow from the next room
shining through
a door cracked open
I step forward,
and in my leaving

is, only,
always,

returning.

END NOTES

1) The lines "I will never leave you or forsake you" and "The coffee's cold and out of reach" in *An Oblivion Like Blasphemy* come from scripture quoting Hebrews 13:5 and Paul Buchanan lyrics in "A Movie Magazine," respectively.

2) The line "there's no place to get to / lovers don't forget you / hello" in *The Fossils I Find* are lyrics to "Telepathic Telepathy" by Nick Jaina.

3) The line "my hands bleed from stitching up torn pretty dreams?" in *Music Education* is a reference to Bruce Springsteen Lyrics in "Racing in the Street," though not directly quoted.

4) The lines "Don't we all see something?" and "Is this the life you always wanted?" in *Drafts* are are lyrics from "A Passing Light" by Shoecraft.

5) The line "I will make a way in the wilderness and rivers in the desert" in *Read Letters II.* is scripture quoting Isaiah 43:19.

ABOUT THE AUTHOR

Katie Scruggs Galloway is a poet, editor, and author of the debut collection *Still and Still Moving*. She is also the co-creator of Becoming // Poetry, a Colorado-based duo that has been writing spontaneous poems for strangers and hosting community writing workshops since 2019. Katie earned a bachelor's degree in English and writing from Eastern Oregon University. When she's not at her desk, you can find Katie creating through analog photography and music (Color Math on Spotify).

Connect with Katie on Instagram:
@k.galloway_

Learn More about Becoming // Poetry
Instagram: @becoming_poetry

ABOUT THE PUBLISHER

Indie Earth Publishing is an author-first, independent co-publishing company based in Miami, FL. A publisher for writers founded by a writer, Indie Earth offers the support and technical assistance of traditional publishing to writers without asking them to compromise their creative freedom. Each Indie Earth Author is a part of an inspired and creative community that only keeps growing. For more titles from Indie Earth, or to inquire about publication, visit:

indieearthbooks.com.

Instagram: @indieearthbooks

INDIE EARTH
PUBLISHING